J
635.9
Bea

Bearce, Stephanie.

A kid's guide to
  making a terrarium.

$29.95

DATE			

Gardening For Kids

A Kid's Guide to Making a Terrarium

Stephanie Bearce

Mitchell Lane
PUBLISHERS

P.O. Box 196
Hockessin, Delaware 19707
Visit us on the web: www.mitchelllane.com
Comments? email us: mitchelllane@mitchelllane.com

Gardening For Kids

A Backyard Flower Garden for Kids
A Backyard Vegetable Garden for Kids
Design Your Own Butterfly Garden
Design Your Own Pond and Water Garden
A Kid's Guide to Container Gardening
A Kid's Guide to Landscape Design
A Kid's Guide to Making a Terrarium
A Kid's Guide to Organic Gardening
A Kid's Guide to Perennial Gardens

ABOUT THE AUTHOR: Stephanie Bearce, who lives in Missouri, built her first terrarium when she was eight years old. She writes: "I used it to hatch a moth cocoon. I let the moth go, but I kept the terrarium. I have been having fun with terrariums ever since. I loved gardens and plants so much that I went to college I took classes in plant science." Stephanie worked as the director of children's education at the Missouri Botanical Garden, where she taught children how to grow plants and how to take care of them. As a science teacher, she has helped her students build terrariums, butterfly gardens, and native plant gardens.

PUBLISHER'S NOTE: The facts on which the story in this book is based have been thoroughly researched. Documentation of such research can be found on page 46. While every possible effort has been made to ensure accuracy, the publisher will not assume liability for damages caused by inaccuracies in the data, and makes no warranty on the accuracy of the information contained herein.

Library of Congress
Cataloging-in-Publication Data

A kid's guide to making a terrarium / by Stephanie Bearce.
    p. cm. — (A Robbie reader. Gardening for kids)
  Includes bibliographical references and index.
  ISBN 978-1-58415-813-4 (library bound)
  1. Terrariums—Juvenile literature. 2. Glass gardens—Juvenile literature. I. Title. II. Series: Robbie reader. Gardening for kids.
  QH68.B43 2009
  635.9'824—dc22
                                    2009001319

Printing   2   3   4   5   6   7   8   9

PLB/PLB2

Contents

Words in **bold** type can be found in the glossary.

Introduction

Building a **terrarium** (teh-RAYR-ee-um) is like bringing a rain forest inside your home. It is fun to pick out plants for your terrarium and watch them grow. You can watch the water in your terrarium as it cycles from the plants to the air and back down to the soil.

Before you begin your terrarium, you must get permission from your family. They can help you find the right container for your home. They will also help you find a safe place for your terrarium. Your family will enjoy watching your plants grow.

When you are choosing your plants, it is important to know how much light they need. Some

plants do not like bright sunshine. Others need a lot of light to grow. You should pick plants that need the same kind of light, then keep your terrarium in that type of light. Put a bright-light terrarium in a window or near a grow light. If you choose low-light plants, keep your terrarium away from windows.

When you buy plants, look at the labels. The label tells the amount of light the plant needs. Seed packets also have that information. It is important to read the labels when you choose your plants. Once you've chosen the best plants for your home and put them together in your terrarium, you will have a living, growing project that you and your family can enjoy for years to come.

Chapter

Chapter

1

What Is a Terrarium?

How would you like to make your own little world? You could plant tiny trees and grow little flowers. You could make curving garden paths. You could make it look any way you want. It would be a secret world all your own.

If this sounds like fun, then you might want to build a terrarium. A terrarium is a sealed glass container used to grow plants. It looks like a tiny world under glass.

Terrariums can be made from many different things. You can use an old glass jar, a flower vase, a fishbowl, or a small fish tank. You can even use a plastic soda bottle. It just has to be clear to let in the sunlight. It must also have a lid to keep the water in. You can decorate your terrarium with rocks and shells.

Terrariums can be very big—even as large as five feet long and three feet tall. Some terrariums are tiny. A little jar may hold only one plant. Most terrariums hold only plants, but some people use terrariums as homes for pets. Snakes and lizards can live in big terrariums called vivariums (vy-VAYR-ee-ums). A viviarium has a lid or door that can be removed to feed the animals.

Fittonias are easy to grow in terrariums, and their pink-and-green leaves are cheerful. When terrariums first became popular in England, people would use them to grow exotic plants and herbs from faraway countries.

Instead of throwing away a bottle or a jar, you can reuse it by making it into a terrarium. You can use clear glass or plastic containers from your trash. You can ask your neighbors for their bottles and jars, or you can visit a recycling center.

People have been growing plants in terrariums for nearly two hundred years. A doctor named Nathaniel Ward invented terrariums. He lived in England in the early 1800s. His hobby was growing plants.

The air in London was very **polluted** (puh-LOO-ted). People used coal for heat. So much coal dust got into the air, the sky turned gray. Plants did not grow well in the dirty air. Ward tried to plant ferns in his yard but they died.

Then he put soil in a glass bottle and covered the bottle with a lid. The plants in the bottle grew.

Modern jars have tight-fitting lids, so it is much easier for you to make a terrarium than it was for Nathaniel Ward. This simple terrarium was made with an old spaghetti sauce jar and an impatiens.

Ward started experimenting with other bottles and plants. He used what he learned to invent a special glass case for plants. It was called a **Wardian** (WAR-dee-an) **case** after him.

During Ward's lifetime, there were no jet planes, so plants were transported on boats. The plants were packed in dark wooden crates. They couldn't get any sunlight in these crates, so most of the plants died. Ward decided to experiment with his Wardian cases. He shipped some plants in a glass case from London to Australia. When the cases were opened in Australia, the plants were healthy. Scientists were amazed. They tried the experiment again. This time they sent plants from Australia to London. The plants arrived healthy again.

Businessmen began shipping their plants inside glass cases. Tea plants were imported to England from China. Banana plants traveled from South America. Plants that were used for medicine were

Terrarium Tip

Large peanut butter jars make good terrariums. They are clear. They also have a wide opening. That makes it easy to put your hands inside. Ask your family to save a jar, or visit your town's recycling center.

You can also grow cacti and succulents in glass containers—as long as you don't overwater them. If there's too much water inside, leave the lid off for a while.

Tropical plants such as the moondrop (tall) and rope plant grow well in terrariums. The warm, wet terrarium has the same climate as the rain forest.

shipped all over the world. Nathaniel Ward's terrariums became famous.

Soon everyone wanted terrariums. They wanted small ones in their homes. They made their own out of glass bottles and jars. Rich people had special terrariums made for their houses. They grew mosses, ferns, and many other kinds of plants. Growing plants in terrariums became a popular hobby.

People still grow plants in terrariums. The plants growing inside glass look pretty. It is like having a little bit of nature inside the house.

You can grow plants in a terrarium, too. You won't have to find a special Wardian case. You can use any glass bottle, then just add soil, water, and plants.

You can use a cookie jar too!

How It Works

In order for plants to grow, they must have light, soil, air, and water. You can put all of these in a terrarium. Plants use sunlight, water, and air to make food in their leaves. This process is called **photosynthesis** (FOH-toh-SIN-theh-sis). The food moves from the leaves to the stems and roots. A plant also needs water. The roots help the plant take up water, then send it to the leaves. The roots also take up extra food and vitamins from the soil.

If you grow plants in a garden, you must watch for **weeds**. Weeds are plants that can choke or kill the other plants. Terrariums are special because they have a lid. The lid keeps out weed seeds, so you never have to weed a terrarium.

Whether they live outside in a garden or inside the house, plants must be watered. However, plants in a terrarium need to be watered only when you build it. This is because a terrarium has its own **water cycle**. A water cycle is how water moves from liquid to gas and then from gas to liquid. Rain is part of the water cycle on our planet.

To recycle its water, the terrarium must have a tight lid. The water cycle begins when water is poured into the soil. When sunlight reaches it, the water will get warm and turn into a gas. This process is called **evaporation** (ee-vah-por-AY-shun). The water gas goes into the air. As it cools, it turns back into a liquid. This process is called **condensation** (kon-den-SAY-shun). The liquid water falls back to the soil as **precipitation** (pree-sih-pih-TAY-shun). We also call it rain.

You can watch the water cycle in your terrarium. You will be able to see water drops on the glass. The water will **condense** (kon-DENTS), or collect at the top. When it gets heavy, it will drop back to the soil. It will rain inside the terrarium.

Terrarium Tip

You can prove that leaves give off water. Find a tree branch with leaves. Put a plastic bag over the leaves. Wrap a rubber band around the opening in the bag. Leave the bag on the leaves for five days, then go back and remove it. You will see water in the bag. This shows that leaves give water to the water cycle. This process is called ***transpiration*** *(trans-pir-AY-shun).*

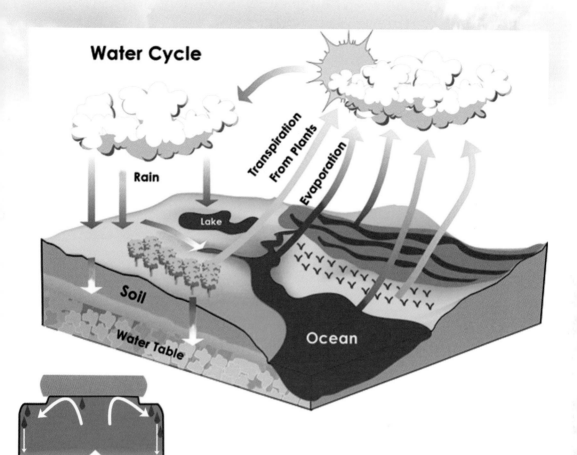

Water Cycle

Rain

Transpiration From Plants

Evaporation

Lake

Soil

Water Table

Ocean

The water cycle works the same way on our planet. Water in the ocean gets hot and turns to water gas, or evaporates. It collects in the sky as clouds. This is called condensation. When the clouds get heavy, the water falls to the earth as precipitation, such as rain.

If you have a tight seal, your terrarium can last for years. Nathaniel Ward had a terrarium that grew plants for 18 years. He never had to weed or water his plants. He just watched them grow.

You can see the water cycle in action in the rain forest. Steam rises from the canopy as the sun warms the rain forest. As it gets higher, the steam cools and condenses. It will fall again as rain.

Have your family help you find a safe place for your terrarium. You don't want it to get knocked over. A strong table or sturdy shelf is a good place. You will need to find a warm, sunny place for it, but do not put your terrarium in a bright, hot window. Keep it away from heaters. Too much sun and heat can kill your plants.

You must also keep your terrarium away from the cold. Windows can get very cold at night. You can protect your plants by putting cardboard in the window at night and taking it out in the morning. This will keep your terrarium plants from freezing.

If a terrarium is too wet it will grow mold, which can kill your plants. If you see mold growing, take off the terrarium lid. Wipe the mold out of the jar. Leave the lid off for a day or two until the soil is dry to the touch. Then you can water the terrarium. Use half as much water as you did the first time. You can always add more water later if the terrarium is too dry.

Tools and Supplies

A terrarium is a **low-maintenance** (loh MAY-tuh-nunts) garden. It does not need a lot of work after it is planted. It is important to build it right, and for that you will need some special supplies.

Although you can use lots of different types of containers for a terrarium, look for a clear jar that has an opening big enough to fit your hand inside. You can make a terrarium with a smaller opening, but you would have to use tweezers, tongs, or sticks to place your plants properly. It is easier to build your first terrarium if you can use your hands. Always make sure the container is clean. Check to make sure there are no cracks or holes.

Make sure you have a lid for your jar, and that it closes tightly. This will seal your container. A good seal will not allow air to get inside the terrarium, which will help your water cycle to work. A plastic lid works better than a metal lid. Metal can rust. The rust can make holes in the lid. This will stop your water cycle from working.

You will need some gravel or small rocks to put on the bottom of your terrarium. The rocks will keep the soil from staying too wet and will leave space in the bottom of the terrarium for air. The air will help the plant roots grow well. Make sure you wash your rocks before you put them in the terrarium.

You will need potting soil for your terrarium. Do not use dirt from the ground. Potting soil has been specially mixed for plants that grow in containers. It is lightweight and has the **nutrients** (NOO-tree-unts), or food, that the plants need. It is also clean. It does not have any **pollutants** (puh-LOO-tants) that can kill plants, such as paint, oil, or soap. You can buy potting soil at any garden store.

You may want to mix some **fertilizer** (FUR-tuh-ly-zer) into your soil. Fertilizer is extra food for the plants that can help them grow and stay healthy.

It's always a good idea to cover your work area with newspaper. It will protect surfaces and make cleanup easier.

There are special fertilizers just for plants in terrariums and pots. You can buy them at a garden store. Read the label to find the right fertilizer. You can also talk to the people who work at the garden store. They can answer any questions you might have.

A funnel is a good tool for working with terrariums. You can pour the soil into the top of the funnel, and it will go into your jar without making a mess. You can buy a funnel, or you can make one out of paper. Just roll the paper into a cone, but leave an opening at the bottom. Tape the cone together, and you've got a funnel.

Terrariums are usually small, so you will not need big shovels for digging. Instead you may want to use a kitchen spoon or a fork. Be sure to ask your family for permission. You don't want to ruin your mom's good kitchen tools.

Terrarium Tip

You can learn more about plants and terrariums by visiting a garden center. The people at garden centers have studied plants. They can give good advice. Sometimes they offer classes on horticulture (HOR-tuh-kul-chur), which is the study of growing plants.

Some terrariums may need a **grow light**, which is a special lightbulb that helps plants grow. It is also called a fluorescent (flor-ESS-ent) light. If you cannot put your terrarium by a window, or if your home does not get a lot of sunlight, a grow light will be a wise purchase. You can buy inexpensive grow lights at the garden store.

If you gather all your supplies—container, potting soil, rocks, plants, and watering can with water—before you start, you'll have your terrarium together in no time.

You will also need a small pair of scissors. You can use them to **prune** your plants. *Prune* means to cut or trim the plants. It is important to keep plants small in a terrarium. If they grow too big, they can die, or they can choke out your other plants. Pruning keeps your terrarium plants healthy and looking nice.

Chapter

4

Choosing Plants

Picking plants for your terrarium can be a lot of fun. **Tropical plants**, which come from warm, wet areas of the world, grow well in terrariums—they're just a lot smaller than the ones in the wild. They grow naturally in rain forests, so they will do well in the warm, damp world of a terrarium.

You need to pick plants that will fit into your container. Plants that grow very big will not work in a terrarium. You should look for plants with small leaves.

Some plants that work well are creeping figs. They have small leaves and grow close to the ground. They will not get too big for the terrarium. Mosses grow well in terrariums, too. They look like a soft green carpet. They can live with very little light, and they like plenty of water. Small ferns have lacy leaves that look great in a terrarium, and they like moist soil. Philodendrons (fih-loh-DEN-druns) have heart-shaped leaves and grow quickly.

Philodendron

Terrarium Tip

Choose a few types of plants that will grow to different heights. Combining short, medium height, and tall plants will make your terrarium look more interesting.

Some plants have **variegated** (VAYR-ee-uh-gay-ted) leaves. This means the leaves have more than one color. They can be green-and-white. They can be pink-and-red. If you want a lot of colors, you might try using Pilea, Fittonia, or Pink Star Cryptanthus.

The Pilea has red in the leaves. It is also bumpy, so it will add an interesting **texture** (TEX-chur), or surface pattern, to your terrarium. The Fittonia has pink, white, and green leaves. It grows well in low light. The Pink Star Cryptanthus has spiky leaves, with red or pink in the middle of the plant.

Some flowers will grow in terrariums. You can plant small begonias (beh-GOH-nyuhs). Begonias have pink, red, or white flowers. You can also grow African violets, which have purple or pink flowers and fuzzy leaves. Small primroses have pink, purple, or yellow flowers.

Miniature African Violet

Terrarium Plants and How High They Will Grow

1-3 inches

Baby Tears

Gloxinia

Cryptanthus

Irish Moss

3-6 inches

Hepatica

Tahitian Bridal Veil

Spider Plant

Watermelon Peperomia

6-12 inches

Aluminum Plant

Maidenhair Fern

Prayer Plant

Bloodleaf

Terrarium Plants for High to Medium Light

Rope Plant

Episcia

Pilea Moon Valley

Iron Cross Begonia

Miniature Sweet Flag

Moss Sandwort

Terrarium Plants for
Medium to Low Light

Swedish Ivy

Philodendron

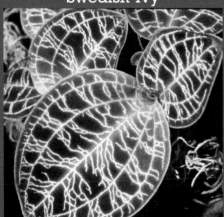
Jewel Orchid

African Violet

Peperomia Fraseri

Blue Peacock Moss

Terrarium Tip

Don't be afraid to experiment. Try growing different plants and seeds. Some of them will grow and some of them will die. When you experiment, you can learn more about plants. You can be a scientist like Nathaniel Ward.

When you pick your plants, be sure to read the labels. The labels give good information about the amount of light and water the plant needs. For most terrariums, you should only pick plants that like damp soil. A terrarium is like a tiny rain forest. It will stay wet. It is not a good place for plants that like to be dry. Cacti can be used in a terrarium if you keep the terrarium dry. Cacti are desert plants and need very little water. A desert terrarium needs only a few tablespoons of water.

You should also find plants that like the same kind of light. Some plants need a lot of light to grow. These plants should be in the sun. Some plants, called low-light plants, like small amounts of light. They should be in a more shaded place.

You need to know where you are going to put your terrarium before you buy your plants. If it will be near a window, you need to buy plants that like bright light. If it will be away from a window, you need low-light plants. You can ask people who are working at the plant store. They can help you pick out the right plants.

Instead of using plants that are already growing, you can also plant seeds in a terrarium. It takes longer for the plants to **mature** (muh-CHOOR), or get big, but it is fun to watch the seeds sprout. Scatter the seeds on top of the soil, then water the soil. Cover the seeds with a light layer of soil. This is a soil blanket for the baby seeds. It will take at least a week for the seeds to sprout.

There are lots of plants that you can grow from seed in a terrarium, such as begonias, impatiens (im-PAY-shuns), coleus (KOH-lee-us), and petunias (peh-TOO-nyuhs). You can also try primroses or geraniums (jer-AY-nee-ums).

Some people use terrariums to start seedlings. When the plants get big, they take them out of the terrarium and plant them in a pot or garden. You can do this if the opening on your terrarium is wide enough to lift the baby plants out.

Petunias

Chapter

Chapter **5**

Building Your Terrarium

The first step in making a terrarium is to line the bottom with rocks or sand. Then you can add the soil. The terrarium should have at least two inches of soil for the roots to grow. If you have a large terrarium, you may want to add more soil. Once you have added the soil, you are ready to put in your plants. Follow the directions on the label for how deep to set your plants into the soil.

Making terrariums is easy and fun. Most people like to make more than one at a time. They like to experiment with different containers and try new plants. They even make terrariums to give as gifts. You may want to try building different types of terrariums, too.

Some people like making mini-terrariums. These are terrariums made with very small jars. Small terrariums are good for people with very little space. They can be kept on a desk or windowsill.

If you want to build a mini-terrarium, look for a small jam or jelly jar. Make sure the lid fits and seals tightly. Wash the jar and take off the label. Then use a funnel to line the bottom of the jar with sand. The sand will work like small rocks to give the roots **drainage** (DRAY-nij)—space for the water to move away from the roots. Add soil, and then add your small plant.

Water the soil until it is damp. Don't put in too much water. If it is too dry, you can add more water in a day or two. You will know if you have enough water by looking for the water cycle. If you see water collecting at the top of the terrarium, then begin to drip, you will know that your water cycle is working.

You can decorate the lid of your mini-terrarium by gluing cloth or felt to the top. Or you can use

To build your terrarium, first choose an attractive, clear jar that your hand will fit inside (1). Put a layer of washed stones in the bottom (2). Gently spoon fresh potting soil (3) into your jar (4). Be sure the soil is deep enough for the roots of your plant, and dig a little hole for them. (If your plants will be too tall, choose a larger jar, or prune with scissors.) Holding each plant close to the base of the stem, gently place it in the hole. Push some soil over the roots (5). Choose some fun little toys to decorate your terrarium (6), add some water and tighten the lid, and you're done (7).

permanent markers to color the lid. Sometimes it is fun to make the lid look like a flower.

Some people like to build very large terrariums out of containers such as old fish tanks. A large terrarium can be fun because you can grow larger plants. Sometimes people keep snakes or lizards in large terrariums. These terrariums take up a lot of

Lizards in a vivarium. Vivariums are hard work, but they can be rewarding. You can create a beautiful habitat for your reptile friends.

You can buy or make furniture to decorate your terrarium. You may want to create a garden scene or build a whole park.

space, and snakes and lizards need special care, food, lighting, and surroundings. You will need help from an adult to take care of the animals. This setup will not work for most people. This type of terrarium has a special lid that can be removed to care for the animals. It must be put back in place to keep the water cycle working.

You might like to make your terrarium look like a **miniature** (MIN-ee-a-chur) world. You can make little park benches out of craft sticks. You can make walking paths with tiny stones. You can even make or buy small houses to go inside your terrarium. Get creative. Think of other things that you usually see in a park. You could make tiny statues or a little birdbath or even a swingset.

To make your terrarium look like a miniature rain forest, you can use plants that look like rain forest trees. You can put moss on the ground to look like the forest floor. You can even buy plastic rain forest animals at the store. Your terrarium could be home for gorillas, monkeys, and jaguars.

These terrariums are decorated with plastic zoo animals to create miniature jungle scenes.

A real gorilla enjoys living in his tropical habitat. You can grow many of the same plants in your terrarium, and add a toy gorilla for fun.

Terrarium Tip

Small plastic animals and toys will not hurt the plants in terrariums. If you build anything for your terrarium, be sure to use waterproof glue. Remember that a terrarium is wet. Anything you put inside must be waterproof or it will fall apart.

If you like castles and dragons, you can put them in your terrarium to create a knight's world. You can build a moat and put in a drawbridge. You might even put in a wizard.

You may want a terrarium that is from another galaxy. You can make your terrarium look like another planet. Find strange-looking rocks. Put in alien creatures. Build a spaceship. Make your terrarium look like Planet X.

You can make your terrarium look any way you want. You just need to use your imagination, and follow the steps for planting a terrarium. If you have a clear container with a tight lid, you can make any world you can imagine.

Use plastic figures and carefully chosen plants to make all kinds of terrarium scenes. Under the man and the lantern, the sphagnum moss looks like tumbleweeds. Under stonehenge, the moss looks like grass. Remember: If you choose to make a desert terrarium, be sure not to overwater.

Crafts

You can decorate your terrarium with rock critters.

All you need are some flat smooth stones, a paintbrush, and some waterproof paint. You can add other decorations, too, like paper eyes or chenille stems. You will also need some old newspapers to cover your work surface.

First, wash and dry the rock. It will need a clean, dry surface for the paint to stick.

Look at your rock and think about what animal or insect you can paint on it. You can use red and black paint to make a ladybug, or gold and black paint to make a tiger or leopard. Maybe you would like to paint a dragon. Be creative.

Once you have finished painting your rock critter, let it dry for a full day. Then give your critter a home in your terrarium.

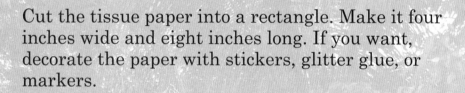

Butterflies love plants, but real butterflies cannot live inside a terrarium. You can use chenille stems, colored tissue paper, and scissors to make a colorful butterfly to sit on your terrarium. Stickers, glitter glue, and markers can make your butterfly sparkle.

Cut the tissue paper into a rectangle. Make it four inches wide and eight inches long. If you want, decorate the paper with stickers, glitter glue, or markers.

Starting on one of the long sides, fold the tissue paper back and forth, like you are making a paper fan.

Wrap a chenille stem around the middle of the paper.

Shape the stem into a butterfly body. Use more chenille stems to make legs and antennae. Unfold the tissue paper and shape the wings. Put your butterfly next to your terrarium. (If you place it inside, the dampness will destroy it.)

 # Further Reading

For Young Readers

Greenwood, Marie, and Sue Nicholson, editors; with Neville Graham, designer. *First Nature Activity Book*. New York: DK Publishing, 2007.

Kalman, Bobbie. *What Is a Plant?* New York: Crabtree Publishing Company, 2000.

Krezel, Cindy. *Kids' Container Gardening*. Batavia, Illinois: Ball Publishing, 2005.

Lawlor, Elizabeth P. *Discover Nature Around the House: Things to Know and Things to Do*. Mechanicsburg, Pennsylvania: Stackpole Books, 2003.

Spohn, Rebecca. *Ready, Set, Grow! A Kid's Guide to Gardening*. Tucson, Arizona: Good Year Books, 2007.

Works Consulted

Carloftis, Jon. *Beyond the Windowsill*. Franklin, Tennessee: Cool Springs Press, 2007.

Courtier, Jane, and Graham Clarke. *Indoor Plants*. New York: Reader's Digest Books, 1997.

Hesayon, D. G. *The House Plant Expert*. London: Expert Books, 2005.

Lavine, Sigmund A. *Wonders of Terrariums*. New York: Dodd, Mead and Company, 1977.

McCreary, Rosemary. *Tabletop Gardens*. North Adams, Massachusetts: Storey Publishing, 2006.

Pleasant, Barbara. *The Complete Houseplant Survival Manual*. North Adams, Massachusetts: Storey Publishing, 2005.

Smith, P. Allen. *Living in the Garden Home*. New York: Clarkson Potter Publishers, 2007.

On the Internet

Enchanted Learning: Pebble and Rock Crafts
http://www.enchantedlearning.com/crafts/pebbles/

Family Fun: Tissue Paper Butterflies
http://jas.familyfun.go.com/arts-and-crafts?page=CraftDisplay&craftid=11038

Kids Garden News: Building a Terrarium
http://www.kidsgardening.com/2006.kids.garden.news/jan/pg3.html

Miniature Garden Shoppe http://www.miniaturegardenshoppe.com

National Geographic Kids: Make a Cool Terrarium!
http://kids.nationalgeographic.com/Activities/Crafts/Miniature-garden

Terrarium Man http://www.stormthecastle.com/terrarium/index.htm

Glossary

condensation (kon-den-SAY-shun)—The process of water gas losing heat and changing to liquid water.

condense (kon-DENTS)—To change from gas to liquid.

drainage (DRAY-nij)—The process of moving liquid away from something.

evaporation (ee-vah-por-AY-shun)—The process of changing from a liquid to a gas.

fertilizer (FUR-tuh-ly-zer)—A food that is added to soil to help plants grow.

grow light—A special lightbulb used to grow plants.

low-light—Needing a small amount of sunlight.

low maintenance (loh MAY-tuh-nunts)—Not needing a great deal of care.

mature (muh-CHOOR)—Adult, or fully grown.

miniature (MIN-ee-ah-chur)—A tiny version of something.

nutrients (NOO-tree-unts)—Food for plants or animals.

photosynthesis (FOH-toh-SIN-theh-sis)—The way plants turn air and water into food using the energy of sunlight.

pollutants (puh-LOO-tants)—The chemicals that hurt soil, plants, and animals.

polluted (puh-LOO-ted)—Made dirty by the use of chemicals.

precipitation (pree-sih-pih-TAY-shun)—Rain, snow, or hail.

prune (PROON)—To cut or trim plants.

terrarium (teh-RAYR-ee-um)—A sealed clear container used for growing plants.

texture (TEX-chur)—The feel of a surface, whether it is smooth or rough.

transpiration (trans-pir-AY-shun)—The passage of water from a plant through its leaves.

tropical (TRAH-pih-kul) **plants**—Plants that grow in the warm, wet areas of the world.

variegated (VAR-ee-uh-gay-ted)—Marked with different patches of colors.

vivarium (vy-VAYR-ee-um)—A terrarium that contains one or more live animals.

Wardian (WAR-dee-an) **case**—A sealed glass case invented by Nathaniel Ward for growing plants.

water cycle—The constant movement of water from gas to liquid through evaporation and precipitation.

weeds—Plants that grow where they are not wanted.

Index